CHRISTINA DEMARA

How
GOD
SAVED
ME

My Mother's Memoirs
ON ABUSE, DEPRESSION
& OVEREATING

Also Written By

CHRISTINA DEMARA

My Prayer Book

Peace is Mine
The Forgiveness Journal

I'm Not Broken
The Power of Prayer, Scripture, and
Interactive Journaling

How God Saved Me
My Mother's Memoirs on Abuse,
Depression & Overeating

The I Am Journal
A Soul-Searching Journal for Creative Women of God

Isaiah 43:2
40 Days of Scriptures, Reflection, and
Journaling for the Lent Season

Meaningful
Books & Resources

Meaningful Leadership
*How to Build Indestructible Relationships with Your
Team Members Through Intentionality and Faith*

Meaningful Leadership Journal

Meaningful Leadership Prayer Book

Meaningful Teacher Leadership
Reflection, Refinement, and Student Achievement

Meaningful Writing & Self-Publishing
*Your Guide to Igniting Your Pen, Faith,
Creativity & Entrepreneurship*

Early Life Leadership
Books & Resources

Early Life Leadership in Children
101 Strategies to Grow Great Leaders

Early Life Leadership
101 Conversation Starters and Writing Prompts

Early Life Leadership Workbook
101 Strategies to Grow Great Leaders

Early Life Leadership Workbook for Girls
101 Strategies to Grow Great Leaders

Early Life Leadership Kids Journal

Early Life Leadership in the Classroom
Resources, Strategies & Tidbits to Grow Great Leaders

CONTENTS

PREFACE

*I*f you like *One Child* by Torey Hayden or *A Child Called It* by Dave Pelzer, you will LOVE *How God Saved Me!* Christina DeMara writes her mother's story of child abuse, depression, and overeating. This story will pull you in and is one of the most severe child abuse cases by multiple family members. These memoirs explain all the obstacles Christina's mother endured including manipulation, sexual abuse, a psychologically impaired mother, and an alcoholic father. Nearly dead inside with the numbness of a sex slave, she prevails, gives her life to God and overcomes depression and overeating. This inspiring story also includes strategies and recommendations on how to overcome depression and overeating.

A Note to the Reader

Dear Valued Reader,

There are many things that happen to us during this God-given life that we just don't understand. I know you, like myself, have questioned: "Why, God?" Over my lifetime, I wasted a lot of time asking why instead of building a relationship with God. Today, I still have a lot of unanswered questions. I still have a lot of pain and I am still afraid of the dark, but one thing I know for certain is that God is in control. I can't let this life be about fear, sorrow, or pain. I felt the need to tell my story to help heal my life and to help heal others. Surviving my childhood and writing this book is something only God could help me do. I don't want my life to be in vain, and I want you to know that no matter what happens in your life, God loves you and is with you. He is our true vindicator. With God, nothing is impossible. This story is narrated by me and written by my daughter. Thank you for reading this book for it is a small glimpse of my soul. Be blessed and keep your eyes on God. ♥

-Christina's Mom

Narration

This book was written by Christina DeMara.

The book reads from the perspective and narration of her Mother telling the story.

IN THE BEGINNING...

was once told, "Tears are a way of healing." tears are flowing as I embark on telling you my story of the little girl that suffered an injustice. She was wronged and wondered where God was. Why didn't anyone rescue her? Where was her mother and father in all of this? Let me start at the beginning, which is where I come from. My background history was given to me by my parents, in which was mostly told by my mother. I was born in Newport, Rhode Island. We were a family of six. I was the youngest of the four children.

My parents were both born in the state of Texas, where they met. My parents married at a young age, and as a navy sailor, my father was immediately shipped out to sea. I don't really think my mother knew what she was in for, or the life she and her children were going to endure. One thing my mom knew for sure was the love of God. She called on the Lord many times and planted Christian beliefs in me.

I remember my mother's parents very well. They were poor and uneducated, but kind and loving. I always felt loved and safe with them. My mother had a primary education of reading, writing, and basic math, but left school at an early age to help support the family, becoming one of the main providers for a household full of kids.

On my father's side, my grandfather died at a very young age. He left my grandmother widowed with their children, including my father. I never really got to know my dad's mother. We visited her, but we never really bonded with her. At a young age, my father went to work in the agricultural fields to help support the family and never completed his education. By the age of 18, he changed the spelling of his last name and joined the United States Navy.

As an adult, my mother confided in me. While she was carrying me in her womb, we lived in Newport, Rhode Island. My father was getting friendly with another woman while my mother was pregnant with me. He was also drinking a lot in those days. The relationship between my parents was fragile, to say the least. He tried to make my mom think she was mentally ill by saying she was not right in her mind. He would often get angry and start calling her crazy. When I think back, it could have been a way to manipulate her and detour the attention of his affair. One day, I think my mom was at a breaking point. We were in the kitchen with nothing on but the light from the top of the oven range. I found myself leaning in and holding my breath while I listened to her story at the kitchen table. She emotionally explained even though she begged him and confronted my father he had continued to see the other woman. My mom felt the woman was a bit on the evil side. She seemed to have some power over my father, my mom explained. In those days, women were not to question anything. She cried and begged him to be the man she married. The man she needed him to be, an honorable husband and father. Protecting himself and the career he built. My father continued to deny any wrongdoing and tried to have my mother admitted to a mental institution. This was not the first time he tried and it was not going to be the last time he tried. It didn't matter to him that she was carrying his child. Nothing mattered to him, but himself.

I was born, March 4th, 1957. My mother said the sky was navy blue and white. It was snowing the night I was born. The roads were gray and covered in ice. My father dropped my mother off at the emergency door entrance as if she was in a hamburger joint drive through. The nurses helped my mom into the hospital carefully, so she wouldn't slip on the ice. As the hospital staff delicately sat her in a wheelchair, they noticed my mom had a black eye. A gift from my dad, the womanizer. This lead me to more questions. "What kind of man hits a pregnant woman? Was I not wanted? Was he trying to hurt me too? Where was God?"

My mom reminded me of Leah in the bible. No matter what she did, it was never good enough for my father. But just like Leah, she was strong and loved God. There are often lies in our head the devil wants us to believe like, "You aren't good enough" and "you can't do any better than the situation you are in now." Don't believe it. God is in control and he can change your life if you let him.

Genesis 29

31 *Yahweh saw that Leah was hated, and he opened her womb, but Rachel was barren.*
32 *Leah conceived, and bore a son, and she named him Reuben. For she said, "Because Yahweh has looked at my affliction. For now, my husband will love me."*
33 *She conceived again, and bore a son, and said, "Because Yahweh has heard that I am hated, he has therefore given me this son also." She named him Simeon.*
34 *She conceived again and bore a son. Said, "Now this time will my husband be joined to me, because I have borne him three sons." Therefore, his name was called Levi.*
35 *She conceived again and bore a son. She said, "This time will I praise Yahweh." Therefore, she named him Judah. Then she stopped bearing.*

THE FAMILY LIFE

*G*oing as far back as I can remember to the age of three; we lived in Texas. My mom was always beautiful, always loving, and always tried to make things right for us. I think she knew our family had problems but tried to make things as normal as she could for us. She took care of us and was never too tired to address our needs. My mom deeply loved her children, she always tried to let us be kids. She loved us, and we felt it every day as we grew up. My dad was very different. He was private, very stern, and demanding. We were all little sailors, and he demanded respect. We were to show it to him by addressing him by his title of Sir or Father Sir. It was a rare occasion when he would laugh or show us any affection as my mother did. My father did not allow or tolerate "laziness." Sometimes it felt like we were in the Navy. We all had to do chores from sunrise to sunset when he was home. He drank in private and usually preferred beer. By the third or fourth one, he was drunk. I even knew at a very early age to stay out of his way when he was drinking. His parenting philosophy was "Children were to behave, and to be seen and not heard."

I remember my brother, who was constantly at odds with my father. As the story goes, from day one of his life, my father had it out for him. My father was extra tough on him because my mom favored him. If it was a life or death situation between my father and brother, my mom would have saved my brother. He could do no wrong in my mother's eyes. He was the "golden child," so they would say. He knew where he stood with my mother and that made him self-righteous and mean. My brother was a tyrant. He was also out of control, and I was just a little girl suffering in silence.

As I look back at myself, I was a very nervous child. Everything scared me, and rightly so with the cold, intimidating family life I had endured from birth. I guess it was an onset from my dad. Whether he was drunk or not drunk, he was always screaming and yelling. From this, any loud sound would startle me immediately. The floor buffer scared me. The vacuum cleaner scared me. Where we lived in Texas, they would have a noon air raid sound go off, and my mom would find me hiding, crying, scared under the table. The sound of an ambulance, firetruck, and thunder would scare me. To this day, I remember sitting in the corner of an open carport. My dad was working on a project with my other siblings. He was yelling and giving each one a direction and lecture on how to do things right.

There I was, curled up in a ball chewing and ripping off my toenails till they bled. My mom came out to calmly ask my dad to stop yelling at us. I was an overly emotional child, and the darkness that loomed over my family didn't help.

There were a lot of things going on in our home that were unhealthy, and that is probably why we never had friends or family over. For the most part, my father kept us on a schedule. We were limited from the public or from growing up with friends of our own. As the drinking went on, so would the arguing. He would always find some reason to be upset at my mother. I was always scared of my dad. I would hold on to my mother in fear as early as I can remember. I knew he was bad, and I was scared for her. I wanted to save her from him. She would put us to bed as he would pass out, and my mom would go to bed clutching on to a prayer book and her rosary.My mother was loving, selfless, and forgiving. Tomorrow was a new day. My mother was always so graceful, but like the saying goes "you never know which way the wind is going to blow" in our house.

It was difficult growing up scared all the time. We all found ourselves walking on eggshells. Our hearts were full of fear and anxiety, and that is not how God wants us to live. In Philippians 4:5-7 it says, 5 Let your gentleness be known to all men. The Lord is at hand. 6 In nothing be anxious, but in everything, by prayer and petition with thanksgiving, let your requests be made known to God. 7 And the peace of God, which surpasses all understanding, will guard your hearts and your thoughts in Christ Jesus.

LOVE, PEACE
& PAPER DOLLS

My next memory is an explosive argument. It was loud and pierced my ears. This time it was my mother and father yelling. The next day, my eyes quickly widened, as I could hear an engine roaring outside. A moving truck came, packed us up, and in the middle of the night, we were on a bus. It was a big silver bus, shiny and bright. I felt something coming over me I didn't feel very often, excitement. We were going on an adventure, I thought. I woke up that morning at my grandparents' home. They didn't have much and lived in the poor part of town. The neighborhood streets were lined with little square wooden cottages with wide porches. All of the paint was old, and what was once white, was now a modest gray. My grandparents rented a little house with a bed in each room, even if it wasn't a bedroom. Although they were poor, there was a sense of peace that came over all of us, even my brother. There was a sense of love and safety.

At last, my mom seemed happy. She glowed as she was surrounded by family members. Her sisters and other family members came to see us. Everyone was happy. There was no yelling, just a warm, joyful home. It was like a big party. Everyone smiled and was happy to see us. I thought it was the most fun thing ever, being around so many happy people. The most exciting thing was everyone lived within a four-block radius. When we finished our daily chores, we would walk block-to-block visiting and playing with cousins. We waited for the Iceman and the watermelon man. We would all just sit there peacefully on the porch with the grown-ups as they exchanged stories and family news. I had a box of paper dolls and my imagination. I felt like a child for once. It was the best time of my life and my mom's life. I had no idea why we were at my grandparent's house, but it felt like a safe vacation. I didn't care why we were there, but eventually, all good things come to an end.

TROUBLE STARTS

One day, we were at my grandparent's house, what seemed like a usual day. The women had done all the chores of cleaning the house and started preparation for a late lunch. The Iceman had passed, and the blocks of ice were in the metal tubs chilling the watermelon to soothe an after dinner sweet tooth. All the adults were all sitting on the porch talking and enjoying one another's company. I was playing with my box of paper dolls. It was raining hard, and I had gotten up to go to the restroom. My mom asked if I wanted her to go with me, and the biggest mistake I made was saying, "No, I am a big girl, I can go on my own." The restroom was at the back of the house. I didn't know my brother was hiding in the restroom. When I walked in, he grabbed me fast. By this time, it started to thunder. I could hear the thunder booming and the lighting filled the sky. The rain poured down on my grandparent's wooden cottage. I couldn't feel or hear myself breathing, but I could hear the laughter of my family outside. He threw me in a small water heater closet and locked it on the outside. It was pitch black. I was frantic. I was crying and screaming. I was pounding on the door. "Why could no one hear me?" Where was my mom, my savior who was always there when I needed her warmth and to feel secure in her arms? The roar of the storm just kept on getting louder. I was soaking wet from my own sweat and tears.

Finally, my grandfather must have wondered what happened to me and came inside the house looking for me. He heard my cry for help and un-locked the door. He was my archangel and rescued me. I ran into his strong big arms as he lifted me up and wiped the wet hair from my face. I could see his face was tight and angry. "Who?" he asked, "Who did this to you?" When I told him, he put me down and said, "sit by your mom". I didn't move. I was exhausted from the fear and yelling for help. My grandfather went for his big, black, thick, leather belt. He took my brother out to the back of the house and whipped him well. That was my first encounter of intimidation and psychological abuse by my brother. I never wanted to be left alone or sleep alone after that. To this day, I can't be in the dark, even if I know its day outside. I need the light. I sleep with a nightlight and leave the door open be-cause the feeling of being enclosed overwhelms me.

Shortly after that incident, we were sitting on the porch at my grandparent's house, and my dad ap-peared in a brand new green car. He drove up like he was in a parade. My mom's eyes were still. I don't think she was expecting him. She rose before he could stop and walked towards the car. We didn't move. He talked to my mom by the car then, he came to hug and kiss us. That is probably the first time I remember him hugging me. The next morning, we got up, dressed, and packed up our belongings. My grandma and grandpa hugged and kissed us. I didn't want to leave. But maybe things were going to be different. Maybe my dad loved us after all. I remember looking out the back of the car window with sadness. The party was over. I was waking up from this dream. My grandparents blessed my mother and gave her a silver pot with a black handle. My grandparents were humble people. That was all they had to give my mom as a gift, and probably one of the only things they had. What little they gave was a blessing. That pot became the bean pot and made the best pinto beans.

Love is a powerful thing. It stays in our soul. Once it's there, it may change but never go away. The love I felt from my grandparents is something I hold on to and strive to give my own grandchildren. In Psalm 71:17-24, the Psalmist paint a beautiful picture of life, age, and what our faith looks like.

Psalm 71:17-24

17 *God, you have taught me from my youth.*
Until now, I have declared your wondrous works.
18 *Yes, even when I am old and gray-haired, God, don't forsake me,*
until I have declared your strength to the next generation,
your might to everyone who is to come.
19 *Your righteousness also, God, reaches to the heavens;*
you have done great things.
God, who is like you?
20 *You, who have shown us many and bitter troubles,*
you will let me live.
You will bring us up again from the depths of the earth.
21 *Increase my honor,*
and comfort me again.
22 *I will also praise you with the harp for your faithfulness, my God.*
I sing praises to you with the lyre, Holy One of Israel.
23 *My lips shall shout for joy!*
My soul, which you have redeemed, sings praises to you!
24 *My tongue will also talk about your righteousness all day long,*
for they are disappointed, and they are confounded,
who want to harm me?

CALIFORNIA, HERE WE COME

We were off, and on to a next adventure. I knew in my heart we would never be back. My mom waved to all the family that gathered to see us off, till all we could see was the dust of the dirt road trailing behind us. I gazed out the rear window of the shiny green car and had my eyes fixed on my grandparents till they disappeared into the horizon. We traveled for days and nights. Only stopping for gas and a restroom break. Then an occasional roadside stand for hamburgers and to fill up a thermos of coffee for my father. When he was tired we stopped at the rest stop for him to sleep for a few hours. Then back on the road we would go. Everything seemed to be okay. Occasionally my dad would raise his voice at my mom, and for us to sit still. We knew better than to be jumping around, but we were kids. We were almost at our new destination. It would be where I would live most of my childhood and adult life. Where I suffered at the hands of my brother and father. We finally made it to California. After a long, hot, sticky drive, we pulled up to the front of a brand-new house. My father was relocated to San Diego, California. The house seemed so big. I was too young to go to school, so I stayed home another school year with my mom, as the others went to school.

Once again, my dad disappeared overseas. All I knew was he was gone, which just meant there would be peace and giggling in the house. All except when my brother was around. He took the place of my dad and was constantly hitting me. This was learned behavior, and without any real examples of what a healthy living environment was, my brother was now part of a destructive cycle. I always felt like it was mostly me he would pick on. His abuse wasn't just an annoying tap either. His hands were heavy like stones, and his smacks and punches hurt me both physically and emotionally. I was ten years younger after all. As he entered his teen years, he tested the waters with everything and anything, including me. I believe at this time in his life he started experimenting with drugs. I was living a hell that I didn't understand. I was confused and in pain.

Meanwhile, as my dad was away, my mom tried to keep us all in line. She managed the house and would teach us about God. She put us all in catechism classes every Saturday morning and church on Sundays. Even though our roots in faith were not planted deep, she tried her best to plant the seeds of

God's goodness in us. We all knew God had a son named Jesus, and Jesus had died for us. I remember seeing a Bible, but this was as much as I knew.

When my dad was out to sea, this gave me the opportunity to get to know my mom better. She was funny and playful. She liked to try new recipes, and on some days, I would get lost with her inside all the newest cookbooks. Although, there was something different I noticed about my mom. I was about six years old at the time, my mom started to show signs of a paranoid schizophrenic. She would say things like "don't say those things loud, people are listening to us," or "they are recording and listening to what we all say, don't talk like that." She was always worried that we were all being watched. One day, I remember walking up to her while she was speaking to the light switch cover.

One day I tried it myself. I said "Hello! Is anyone there? If someone is listening to us like my mom says so, please listen to this! I want a new bike for Christmas!", and she panicked. I was just joking and playing as kids do, but the panic on her face was so great. It was burned into my mind, and I still remember it. She called me by my full given name and said: "stop right now, they are going to come and take us away, and your dad will make sure we never see each other again." After seeing the fear in her eyes and hearing the pain in her voice, I never played around like that again. The fear on her face left me with two thoughts. The first was, "my mom was not well", and the second was "what kind of monster was my dad, that he caused my mom such fear of being watched and listened to?" She always feared being taken away from her children because that was something he always threatened her with.

John 10:10
The thief only comes to steal, kill, and destroy.

Time passed but my brother never changed. Nothing in our house ever changed. He found amusement and satisfaction in being cruel. For instance, he had a game he called "peel". We had a long hallway with bedroom and bathroom doors across from each other. He would position himself at the end of the hallway with several rubber balls. When he yelled "peel" we had to run down the hall, and he would throw a fastball and hit us with it. You had to be fast and run to the next door on either side of the hall. He continued to throw the balls. To be hit with one of the rubber balls, going at a fast spin, the hit would sting and burn you. If you didn't run from door to door, he would come and get you and drag you out. We had to go along with him, because either way, you were going to get it. I had rationalized it wasn't so bad if you voluntarily went along with him.

You may ask where my mom was while all this was happening. Back in those days, it was not illegal to leave your kids home while you went to pay the water bill or run errands. My mother left us with my brother because he was the only boy. It didn't do any good to tell on him because she was blind to any wrongdoing he did. He could have done some wrong in front of her, and she would still defend him or make excuses for him.

When my dad was around, if we told my dad, all hell would break loose. My dad would get all ugly with my mom, yelling vulgarities, and my mom would still defend my brother. Then the guilt I felt, to see her get yelled at because of him. I learned not to go down that road. That was the first and last time I tattled on my brother to my dad. I just stood there next to my mom. I clung to her side as she cried, and I was scared and confused. It was like being awake in the middle of a nightmare. Later, I could hear her pray, "God help me"; it broke my heart. When it came to my brother, I learned to keep my mouth shut because I did not want to put my mom through that abuse again.

THE BROKEN GIRL

I was about seven years old when I put pieces of the puzzle together. When my father was gone, it was a calm and peaceful feel over the house. When he was home we were tense and walked on eggshells. He was the commander-in-chief. We were his crew, doing and saying as he commanded. It was about this time that my dad was participating in what was called a "tour" of 2 to 3 months of deployment out to sea. He called it "west pack". The ships would go out to sea for a short period and return. Nothing could have prepared me for the hell that was about to be unleashed on me. It was summertime and I wasn't sure where my sisters were. My mom left to do errands and said she would be right back. I begged her to take me, and she said I would be alright and that my brother was to watch me. I didn't like that idea, but she promised to bring me a surprise and left.

Shortly after that, my brother had a surprise for me. He grabbed me and took me to the middle bedroom. He pulled me into the closet and pulled my pants down and began to have sex with me. I had no idea what was happening, and he put his hands over my mouth. He had his way with me till he was done. I was crying. My face was wet with tears. Where was my mom? Why did she leave me with this monster again? I knew enough, that what he was doing to me was wrong. As he pulled his pants up and got off me, his words were "I swear if you tell anyone, you will be sorry" and "it will just be worse for you. I promise you." I said, "I will tell mom" and his self-righteous response was "She would not believe you. She will believe me over you". I knew she favored him over my dad. He was probably right and then I said, "when dad comes home I will tell dad" and his answer to that was "what so he can yell at mom for not taking care of you and maybe even hit her." He said the keywords. These were things that I did not want to happen to my mom, to be yelled at once again by my dad, possibly beaten or admitted to a mental hospital. I loved my mom more than myself. I already knew she was not mentally stable.

As I look back, I can see her breaking down from all the verbal, emotional, and physical abuse. I thought if I tattled on my brother this would be the ammunition my father needed to hospitalize my mother. I felt like he was always looking for a reason to take her away. Just thinking about her being taken always felt like a thousand knives in the heart. I knew I would never see her again. If my mom was gone, I'd have to live a miserable life with my dad and my brother. I was stuck like a mouse in a trap. My brother had me in the palm of his hand. After he got away with sexually abusing me once, and he didn't stop. I turned into his sex slave. He would do with me what he wanted, when he wanted, and that was the start of hell in my life. I would lay there lifeless like a rag doll, dead inside but still breathing. I not only wondered where was my mom to save me, but even more, where was that God she taught me about and his son Jesus that loved all the little children? Then I thought, did they love all the small children like my brother who was abusing me sexually? My head was always spinning with thoughts. I was a confused little girl. I was broken and trapped.

One day I got brave, and I asked him "Why are you doing this to me?" His response was this, "It's what married people do to show their love to each other, and I'm showing you my love for you." Immediately, I thought this is not right. He is sick and crazy. We weren't married, and I never showed him any affection. Not even as a sibling. When my parents were around I would try to pretend he was invisible. Another time he got ahold of me and was having sex with me, I started to bleed, and I began to scream and cry. He calmed me down and told me that it was natural and that I was no longer a virgin, and I was his and only his. I look back and wonder why I was never rescued. How was he never caught? When is this going to stop? Every time he had his way with me sexually or beat me up, he got away with it. I never told anyone. Not one soul because the idea of losing my mom was unbearable. She was the only glimpse of light and security I had in my life.

Eventually, my brother got himself into some trouble. I don't know what he did, but he ended up going away. He had to do time at an all-boys detention camp, out in the middle of nowhere. Literally, just flat dirt land. It was to my understanding from my father's comments, "it was where the worthless, nothing, nobodies go. Those boys are never going to amount to anything." Hearing my father make those comments, I felt like there was just a little justice served.

Then one day, my brother appeared back home. Being in an all-boys detention camp did not do him any good because he came back worse. Ten times meaner, and I spent most of the day trying to avoid him, at all cost. When he came home from the detention camp, he was smoking pot and popping pills, mostly barbiturates or downers. He would just sit there and stare into space. After all of that with him, you would think "what more could happen?"

Well, it was a weekend, a Friday night. My dad came home and started with the beer after dinner. Usually, after a 6 pack, if he had not found any little thing to yell at us kids and my mom for, he would go to sleep. He then would wake up at 4 am. In silence, we could hear everything going on in the house. I often heard my dad rustling in the kitchen. We learned to play possum and lay in bed. We'd lay still like we were asleep, till he called roll call. Suddenly, you could hear that noise, which meant it was not going to be a good day. The pop sound of him opening his first beer at 4 am. On this particular day, he had my mom dress us up to go to his company picnic, at a large local park. One thing that I knew about the company parties from the Navy is they went all out. It was going to be fun, so I was excited to go. He was going to take us all, except my mom. I don't know what his reason was for not taking her. On our way to the park, he was already numb and drunk. So drunk he had my oldest sister driving. It was my brother and my other sister in the back seat. My oldest sister driving, me in the middle of the front seat, and my dad on the passenger side drinking a beer. We were on the highway part of the road, and he began to kiss me. Kissing me on the lips and hugging me. I thought this is not like how a dad is supposed to kiss his child. My oldest sister got mad. She told him "if you don't stop I will pull the car over." He let me go but started to yell at her to keep driving.

We got to the picnic, and he just turned us loose in this big park. There was so much going on, my brother took off. My oldest sister tried to watch out for my sister and me. At the same time, we were watching my dad as he continued to drink the afternoon away. The beers just kept coming. There were massive tubs of ice with kegs of beer and soda pop bottles. There were hot dogs, hamburgers and

T-bone steaks. Cases and cases of chips, but none of the food interested him as much as the beer. After what seemed to be a long afternoon, he rounded us up, and we went home. My sister watched his every move. He looked like he was going to pass out when we arrived home. He went to the room and began playing the stereo. That was one thing he liked to do. When he was drunk he liked to play the record player very loud, and that day was nothing different. He was drunk, and the music was playing loud, my mom sent me to the bedroom with a cup of coffee. I knocked, and he opened the door. I brought in the coffee to him, and he closed the door. He put the coffee down and picked me up to dance in his arms. He then began to grope me and kiss me, and it was an instant flashback of when my brother said: "this is what married people do". All I remember was my dad pulling my dress down and said: "don't say one word of what just happened." I could not understand why this was happening to me again. He opens the door, and my oldest sister saw him. Later that evening his eyes lit up with fire. I think he had remembered my sister protecting me in the car. He was not done with her for telling him to leave me alone in the car. My dad yanked her to the room and beat her for protecting me earlier.

After my many sexual encounters with my brother and the one-time encounter with my dad, my life seems to be a blur. I just tried to get through each day of my life. No matter what, I was always trying to watch out and protect my mother from my father, never leaving her alone. In my own way, I felt like I had become her protector, instead of her being mine. I saw her slowly spiral into a shadow of the glowing woman that she once was. She was now a gray shadow of a women. I didn't want her locked up in a mental institution. She was the only healthy love I knew.

My dad, I learned his patterns and everyday habits. It was safe to say, I knew when he was coming home drunk or not. I knew what to say to him to please him, so he would not start yelling at my mom for something I said or did. I knew when to just leave him alone. I would pray to God he would just pass out in the room. My mom would send me in the room to turn off the loud music. If he did not wake up, that meant, we were safe for that night from him. We would sit in the dark, my beautiful mom and I, waiting for the older kids to come home from the football game. We'd eat popcorn with the TV on low to not wake him.

From all of this trauma in my life, I did not turn out to be a perfect child. As I look back I was very lost and just coping. I blocked out what my brother and dad did to me. My mom, my love for her was so great and knowing she was not mentally stable, how could I be angry with her? As an adult, I wondered what would've really happened if I told my mom about my brother and father. I knew that could be the start of worst things to happen. Would things of been different then? How they planted in my head that she would have reacted in their favor. You can't go back and change things. I knew I couldn't change my childhood. I knew I couldn't change my family. I just felt like I always had so many unanswered questions.

In Daniel 10:10-13 an angel comes to him in a time if pain. The scripture says, "Behold, a hand touched me, which set me on my knees and on the palms of my hands. 11 He said to me, Daniel, you man greatly beloved, understand the words that I speak to you, and stand upright; for am I now sent to you. When he had spoken this word to me, I stood trembling. 12 Then he said to me, don't be afraid, Daniel; for from the first day that you set your heart to under-standing, and to humble yourself before your God, your words were heard: and I have come for your words' sake. 13 But the prince of the kingdom of Persia withstood me twenty-one days; but, behold, Michael, one of the chief princes, came to help me: and I remained there with the kings of Persia.

There is evil out there because we live in a fallen world. Daniel was in emotional pain and cried out to God. This verse says God heard him the first time he prayed. I knew God heard my prayers, but where was he? As I look back, I see that I was weak in my faith. I have since learned that God will vindicate me. Like in this verse, Daniel had no idea that there was a battle going on, but God always prevails.

THE DOMINO EFFECT

As I reflect, my life seems like one big domino effect because of my sexual abuse. I was looking for love and approval. I just wanted to be valued. With all the dysfunction and abuse, made me feel like trash. I always felt shamed and broken. The love I was shown was not the love of God, but the love of a monster that was not real. The person I was then was lost, confused, and mentally ill because of the abuse I endured as a child, and the poor choices I made trying to cope.

As I reached the high school years, I found myself making bad choices. My father would drop me off at the front door of the school, and I would go out the back gate with my girlfriends to ditch school. I was growing up in the late 60's and early 70's. I felt like things could not get any worse at home. It seemed no matter how hard I prayed, nothing was going to change. My dad was still going to come home late from work and drunk.

One summer afternoon, I was out with a girlfriend in the neighborhood. My other friend invited us to the park to smoke some marijuana and it just seemed like the thing to do. That was my first experience with drugs. I had also become aware of my body image. I just wanted to look good. I started to save my lunch money to purchase drugs at school to lose weight. I wanted to lose the extra pounds that I had put on from emotional eating. At home, during those times, food was homemade with butter and often cooked in lard. I also had gained weight from craving junk food from the marijuana smoking. Sometimes our thoughts and insecurities take us down the wrong path. I was feeling a lot of pressure. It was my last year of school, my dad had started in on me. Daily, he'd ask "What are you going to do with your life?" He was nagging me like a record on repeat.

I got home, and there was my dad with a beer in his hand. He was scolding my mom for something while she was cooking in the kitchen, and when I was high it just didn't really matter. Nothing did. I found out real fast that drugs were an escape from the reality of all the noise in my head and every-thing that was going on inside our house. The good, the bad, and the ugly. We'd go to meet other boys that we liked from another rival high school and get high. I just did not care about anything, but at the same time, I didn't want to get caught. Only because, it would be my mom who suffered for my misbe-having. So, I was always aware of my surroundings, and I knew when to stop.

One day, I ditched school with the girls and fell

in love. He was twenty years older than me, but he caught my eye. He was handsome, and there was something about him that I just wanted to know more about. We flirted back and forth with comments and somehow out of the conversation, I landed a date with him to the local drive-in movie theater. I was so excited, but my worry was how was I going to get out of the house to see him? Our date was for Friday night, and in the late afternoon, I had made plans with him to pick me up at the park. Yes, I was going to sneak to see him. I was 17, and he was 34 soon to be 35; he could not just knock on my front door and ask to take me out. He had bought beer for him and a bottle of gin for me with some soda to drink. We were talking and watching the movie, and he started to make advances towards me. I was nervous at first, thinking "what had I gotten myself into?" I wanted him to slow down because I was not that type of girl that was fast and easy. I just kept thinking in the back of my mind, he wants to do me as my brother did. I told myself it's not going to happen! The shoe was on the other foot now, I considered myself still a virgin. No matter what my brother and dad had done to me. It was going to be my decision whether or not I wanted to have sex with him. I chose not to, I wasn't ready for that. He ended up taking me home.

On the drive home I noticed, it only took this guy like three beers and he was getting ugly like my dad. He dropped me off, and before I got off the car he said to me "I don't know what kind of games you are playing, but there are ladies that are willing to give it to me for nothing!" My reply, "That's fine! There is a phone booth across the street, why don't you go and call them?" He took off, and I went in the house. I was a little disappointed with the outcome of the date or what I thought was a date. Part of me kind of liked him, I didn't know why. Maybe because he showed me attention? Shortly after he left me at my house, the phone rang in my bedroom. I answered it, and it was him. He apologized and said, no one had ever turned him down. I forgave him, and we planned to have lunch the next day.

I met him at the park again by my house. We went to his favorite diner to eat hamburgers. We talked, and got to know each other. I found out his parents were alive and lived in the next town over from me. He had a sister who was married and had children. He was divorced with two kids from a previous marriage. Our relationship got serious over a year. I got to know him as a man and as a father. He had a big part in raising his two children. Later in our relationship, come to find out there was a third child and possibly a fourth. What did I get myself into? Soon after, I got pregnant, then there was our daughter, Christina. After she was born, I realized that he was just like my dad. I tried to rationalize it. I would start to tell myself "so what if he drank a little like my dad, my mom stayed with my dad after all these years. If she could, so could I."

People would look at us funny, like "look at that old man with that young girl." Looking back, it was the love and attention that I did not get from my dad. Maybe I was looking for a father figure of my own, in some way. I do believe he loved me for me, and not in the sick twisted way that my father and brother did.

My real dream in life was to go into the Navy. I wanted to see the world and get a free education. I wanted to become a surgical scrub nurse. Well one day, I saw a commercial for a trade school came on the television. It was for becoming a dental assistant in just 3 short months. I thought, "the answer to my prayers." It was a respectable job and I felt my dad would go for that. I called the school and made an appointment for my dad and me to go. When he arrived from work I was so excited to tell him we had an appointment for me to start in 2 weeks. It was not exactly what he had in mind for me, and he did not let me forget the cost of the school. Two weeks later, I started. I was happy and at the same time, my boyfriend was happy for me too.

For the first time in my life, my world seemed normal and perfect.

As I look back, I never fixed or dealt with my problems. I was in a relationship with a man who was old enough to be my dad. He was divorced with kids. I was taking diet pills and laxatives to deal with the weight. I think I felt okay because I was no longer being abused. I didn't have an authentic relationship with God, but I had a little girl to raise and she brought me joy.

THE SEASONS OF LIFE IN ADULTHOOD

One day, mom asked my oldest sister to help her get an attorney to get a divorce. After thirty plus years of marriage, my sister had helped her. My father came with his tail between his legs and begged her back. My sister hesitated, but my mom told her this time it was over. She was done, and so was I. As I reflected on my mother's life, I started thinking "what was I doing to my daughter?" I realized that I was raising her in the life that I had lived at home. I grew up with an alcoholic, and now my daughter was growing up with an alcoholic. I decided to leave the relationship I was in with Christina's dad. There was no amount of money, no amount of expensive dinners, and no amount of shopping sprees that could keep me there. I was tired of it! At that point, I asked God to help get me out of this situation. Both my mom and I were ready to leave our toxic relationships, and it was a new season in both of our lives.

My dad remarried shortly after the divorce. He also retired from the United States Navy after thirty years. He went to night school and graduated with his high school diploma. Even with this accomplishment in his life, to me, it didn't mean anything after the abusive life I had lived. He got a job at a power plant of a hospital near where we lived. Soon after that, he became ill with asthma. He had called me the day he died. He told me he wasn't feeling well. I told him he needed to go over to the hospital to get checked out. He said he was going home to eat breakfast, shower, and dress and he'd have his wife take him. He never made it to the hospital. While she was driving him, he took his last breath and was pronounced dead as she arrived at the hospital with him in the car. He was young, 65. He died never getting a chance to enjoy life or his kids like the way he should have. He never got the chance to love and appreciate my mom. His sins shackled him and we all paid the price. My mom came to live with me and my daughter because, at the end of my dad's life, he was worried about my mom. He made me promise to take care of her. I would have done it, promise or no promise, as I had done all my life.

Two years later, it was an unusual day for me. I was at work, I went in early to get ahead of my work week. For some reason, I was worried about my mom. It was after 3 pm and had not heard from her all day. She finally called me and sputtered "come quick, your brother is in trouble." I found out the police were with her at his apartment and immediately I went to be with her. I walked into the apartment, and the smell made me sick to my stomach. I quickly stumbled outside to vomit. The officer let me gather myself and then showed me to the restroom to identify my brother. He then continued to fire questions at me. He asked questions about my brother's drug use. He was asking about my mother's mental stability because even though there was evidence of drug use, she did not want to accept it. It looked like he got sick and tried to make it to the restroom and collapsed. My mom told the officer he had a brain aneurysm. My brother was dead at 35 from a heroin overdose. It was my mom who found him days later in a stench-filled bathroom. It was the smell of death.

My mom defended him to his death. That canceled out all thought that maybe if I had told her about the abuse, she would have done something. There were so many thoughts and emotions running through my head and body. I was angry with my mom for being in denial and defending my brother. I will tell you this, I felt saved and freed, but my heart was hurting for my mother and the family he left behind.

The beliefs and the seeds that my mom planted in me were about putting your faith in God. To love each other and honor the Ten Commandments. I remember her telling me "to forgive to be forgiven" and that "God is the redeemer" and "God will punish those who do you wrong." My thoughts were, God had taken both my brother and dad at an early age. They suffered at their time of death. Did God do that to make what they did wrong in my life right and to give me the rest of my life to live out in peace and free of them? I often wondered, "Why does God do what he does?" No one knows.

FINDING MYSELF

*O*ne of the biggest mistakes I made looking back was trying to take control of my life. I was trying to control my life, my emotions, and my daughter. I had to find an inner peace because I knew I had issues. After the deaths of my father and brother, I finally found the courage to tell someone and their response was "Why are you telling me now? They are dead!" I felt like this person thought I was lying, so what good was it to say anything to anyone? All I knew was this little girl was robbed of her innocence. Could I get it back? No. Could I ever process legal charges? No, they both passed away. I felt like they died, and they got away with it! Every day was a struggle to try and not look back. It was a roller coaster of emotions. I was so depressed. I filled this hole with food, shopping sprees, and things to make me "happy" in the moment. Somedays I couldn't get out of bed and some days I didn't want to come home. I was struggling. I had this little girl and I was just existing in my regular routine that consisted of eating, sleeping, and taking care of Christina.

There were many consequences of trying to take control of my life. I was slowly gaining weight. I was in debt. My daughter was growing quickly without me. The years passed, and I now see I was getting older, and increasingly ill, physically, mentally, and emotionally. After being laid off from my job, I had an emotional breakdown. I was spiraling down, and I was tired of getting back up. I was in a deep depression, so deep I never saw a way out. I felt sad, paranoid, scared to leave my house. I found myself at a psychiatrist office. I just wanted to die and let the earth swallow me up whole. I no longer cared about anything. After an intervention with the doctor, he entrusted me into the hands of my oldest sister. They let me go on my own with several prescriptions. I was diagnosed with Manic Depression, Bipolar, Schizophrenia, and I was at risk for possible suicide. I had a long road ahead of me to heal myself. I always felt alone, empty, and numb to everything for a long time. I was just existing, taking up space with no life inside me. I had finally hit rock bottom.

Some of you might be wondering where my daughter was in all this. My mom was always there for me and Christina. The tables had turned, and she was now taking care of me. By the grace of God, his hands over me and my daughter. I clutched on to her; she was the one thing I hadn't let go of. I entrusted her to my mom most of the time. Even though I would still provide all the necessities for her life, I tried to give her as much attention as I could as I tried to fight my way out of the darkness. I knew if it wasn't for God and his unconditional love for me, I would have lost her during all this craziness too. She had to grow up fast and at an early age. But my mom was relentless and stood next to me as I fought my depression. I tried my best to take an interest in everyday things. A daily routine helped me get through the day. I remember getting Christina dressed for school and dropping her off. Then I would go to my mom's and sleep. I was deeply depressed, so I slept all morning and afternoon, and my mom would watch over me. I would get up and eat. It would be carbs to the max: a big plate of white rice and ground beef with a brown flour gravy. I would eat two huge plates, then go back to sleep. At 3 pm, I would pick up Christina from school. I'd shower her, we would eat dinner, and then she would sit and watch television. I would sleep some more. I'd wake up again, get something to eat, then Christina and I would get ready for school the next day. I was always so exhausted and asleep by eight. The same routine would continue the next day, over and over. I was only sleeping and eating.

One day, I had an appointment with my doctor. I would always ask her, "When will I feel human again? When will I feel like I have life in me?" Every time I asked, she would reply "In time, you will feel like you again." In time? I thought "what does she mean?" By the time that happen, I won't have time left; I want it now! I had to get better, I had things to do and I wanted my life back! I would go home to my mom's and ask her for a big plate of steamed rice and slept on the couch. Food became my medicine. I would eat a lot of white rice or a big plate of spaghetti and sleep. I was turning to food, not to God.

40 YEARS OLD &
500 POUNDS LATER

It was the weekend, and I was in the kitchen. My daughter was playing, and I was in the living room cleaning, moving things around. The sunlight shined bright through the window, and as I looked up, I felt something. I felt a spark of life. Like a car with an ignition that would not turn over and finally, the car started. I truly believe in that moment God was with me. It was a brief period, but I moved forward because I felt Jesus touching me. I continued with counseling, but I was still profoundly depressed. I was still sleeping for long periods of time and consuming large plates of carbohydrates. I had no interest in my appearance besides a hairbrush and a toothbrush, and a shower every other day. The weight piled on and on. I had done a lot of damage to myself and I knew it was going to take time to change and heal. Satan had me believing I was not worthy of anything, and there was nothing good in my life. He had me believing I was doomed from the start by being molested, unwanted, and un-loved. The one thing that Satan couldn't take from me was my love for God.

Christina grew up quickly. She married a Navy sailor and gave birth to a baby boy. That baby was a seed of change God put in my life. I was waking up from the heavy slumber of depression. Christina's new life brought a lot of joy to me and my mom. She ended up moving to Texas to build a new life. Being away from her and the baby quickly left me depressed once again. She told me "Mom I need you alive." She said if I couldn't do for myself, I needed to do it for her and the baby. I was only 43 and I needed to live.

As I reflected on what my daughter said, I went through the many reasons why we eat. "What are my reasons?" I knew I needed to get to the root of mine. We eat when things are good! We eat when things are bad. We eat to celebrate, and even when someone dies. At this point and time of my life, it became a way to cope and ease the emotions I was still harboring. I was addicted to eating. It became like a drug that overpowered me and controlled every part of my being. Eating to comfort myself is something that I will deal with all my life. I remember being 5 years old and crying, and my mother's words were "Eat this, it will make you feel better." I realize the food I sought was carbohydrates, in any form. If I just ate a plate of it, I was going to feel better and it was going to make everything better. By the year

2000, I was at 500 pounds. I had dug myself into a hole and I could not see any way out.

MY LIFELONG JOURNEY TO WEIGHT LOSS

One day I went to the doctor and she talked to me about a high-tech surgery that can help me lose weight. My first thought was, "What if I don't wake up?" I was scared, but at this point, it was my best option. I underwent and survived a successful gastric bypass that year. I had a long road ahead of me with my weight loss journey and believe me, it wasn't easy. After my bypass, I ate nothing but soup broth for the first few months. I was able to start losing weight for the first time, in a long time. It started to boost my energy levels, but my depression still got the best of me. By the end of that year, my mom and I packed up and moved to Texas to start a new life with Christina. It was about time too; I needed change. I remember when she picked me up from the airport, I could not walk. I was in a wheelchair because I was still overweight.

My mom passed away on September 29th, 2005. She was rushed to hospital from the nursing home as I had gone to check on her. My daughter met me in the emergency room, and she passed away in our arms with a smile on her face. I did not only lose my mom, but I lost my best friend. A part of me was gone. I was like a child giving up my security blanket. It was just me and my daughter. Not to long after, Christina found herself in a huge custody battle. All these things took a toll on me, and before I knew it, the emotional eating had set in again. I started to eat to "feel better" again. I was eating to soothe the pain of losing my mom. I missed her every day; I was falling again. I found myself eating to relieve the pain of seeing my daughter's family ripped from under her feet. My new battle was the rage and bitterness over an injustice my daughter and grandkids suffered for the selfishness of one person. After picking up the pieces of our lives, once again, going through every day one day at a time, some of my days were better than others. There were many "Monday diets" and some lasted till Wednesday and most till Monday at lunchtime. Something started to click in me, and it was God calling me. It had been a lengthy process and long overdue. Over the last ten years, there was a change going on inside me. Through my faith and reflection, I had come to four realizations:

1. *I need to let my past go.*

2. *I need to learn forgiveness. This was the hardest for me because I am what my pastor calls a "scorekeeper". I held on to the wrongs in my life and of my Mom's and Christina's.*

3. *I had to forgive myself for all the wrong choices I made, and for all the things I did and didn't do in life. It only took me two water baptisms. The first baptism was in March of 2012.. I said "God, here I am. I need your help and I'm surrendering once again. I'm a size 26-28. I am shameful, and I don't want to get any bigger." I felt myself slipping into this dark hole again and I was desperate to hold on to God. I knew He was the only one strong enough to help me.*

4. *I need to stop trying to control everything. The need for control stressed me out and the stress made me want to eat to feel better. I had prayed for what I have no control over.*

In October of 2017, in private with some dear friends who are missionaries, I was baptized again. This time it was different, I was really ready. As the pastor pulled me under with water I could hear God say, "This is My daughter with whom I am pleased with" and all my shame and guilt was cast out into the deepest parts of the ocean. I felt God speak to me "Go back to the beginning." I didn't know what that meant. What came to mind was my many attempts to lose weight. When the scale went down, I realized I was measuring all my food portions. "Okay Lord!" I thought, "I can do this again". So that is what I did. I measured everything and realized I was eating way over my portion size.

Back in January 2015, I started using measuring cups. I lost 25 pounds, but I was at a standstill. I bought a well-known diet meeting, where you pay once a month and go to weekly weigh-ins. I lost 50 pounds, but that did not last long. I had too many questions in my head. A girl at the meeting gave me a name of a podcast. The person who did the podcast had a private community of ladies from all over dealing with all types of eating issues. Some maintaining, some trying to lose weight. I took the leap and signed up with her. It seemed like the questions I had, she had all the answers. Her story was close to my story, and the story of all the other ladies. For accountability, because I had issues with the weight scale, I joined another weight loss group. I weighed in once a week. Now I'm safe on my own because I have obtained the desire to hold myself accountable.

I now understand weight loss because it's not about the food, it's about the data, measuring, and counting calories. Knowing my data helps me get me through each day. My total weight loss for 2017 was 75 pounds. From 278 to 203. My goal was to lose one hundred pounds. I started having trouble, so I went to see my old gastric medical doctor. I had my surgery in California and when I arrived in Texas, I now needed to get in contact with a local bariatric clinic close by, so I could stay healthy and continue to progress.

In 2017, I went back to see her. She was impressed by my weight loss and explained that many people gain the weight back because they don't change their lifestyle. I asked her for help with my last 25 pounds. She motivated me with praise and suggested I needed a tummy tuck. She explained I had an apron of skin from my stomach and it needs to be removed. I have approximately 25 pounds of skin and weight hanging. She explained, if I have it removed, it would put me at my weight loss goal of 100 pounds. It took me a while to get used to that thought.

I had a lot to think about. I self-reflected and prayed. I wondered, can I find peace with myself if I don't get a tummy tuck done? Can I accept my body 100 percent ultimately the way it is? The other thing is how bad do I want the surgery? Was it enough to get into debt? It was a big concern for me because I was so focused on paying off my bills.

We will see in the upcoming year 2018 when I make an appointment with the doctor to discuss my issue of the tummy tuck. I have questions I'd like to get answers to. I am also praying about it and seeking the guidance of God. Every day in this journey that I have started for the last and final time since January of 2015 is a struggle. The only way I have made it this far is with the strength of God and Jesus Christ and my family. They are there to cheer me on in the good times and not so good times of my everyday struggles. I know now that the issues that I have with food are emotional and indeed are more along the lines of food addiction. I was having a conversation with a friend about this thought of food addiction and I asked her "If God could wipe me clean of a drug addiction overnight, why can he not wipe me clean of this food addiction?"

It had me thinking. Maybe he wanted me to get to the root of my problems. The forgiveness of myself and all the shame in my life. Maybe He wants to peel off the layers of the pain. I had suffered most of my life, and little by little, God saved me. Through my faith, I peeled back and shed the pain, the anger, the confusion. By coming to God, I was able to grant myself the grace I need to stop being the victim and to finally see the bright light of Jesus my lord and savior.

HOW GOD SAVED ME

This humble book is a small look into my life. It seems my past life was always a blur because I had so many issues and problems I was trying to fix, deny or ignore. I wish I could give you a dramatic ending. But the truth is even though I suffered a lot throughout my life, God saved me every day. He saved me when I was in my mother's womb and my father was beating her. When I look back, I now see all the times God saved me, comforted me, and provided for me when I should have been dead or when I thought about hurting myself. God has saved me from conception, and dead or alive he will continue to save me and keep me. Why? Because he has a purpose for my life and for yours too. My testimony of God greatness and his love for me is one many can relate to. No matter how bad things were, I knew there was a great father that would open his arms and lifted me out of the furnace of hell to the stream of the living water to follow his son Jesus Christ. I will spend the rest of my life as a disciple of his people and share my story of His everlasting love because he saved me from abuse, depression, and overeating. This is my testimony on how he saved me.

LIFE LESSONS LEARNED

1. *The biggest lesson I learned was to go to God for all your needs. God is bigger than my abuse, depression, and food addiction. He loves us and wants to help us.*

2. *Seek God in all aspects of your life. Don't just seek him in times of need.*

3. *Try to make each day a better one than yesterday.*

4. *I do not need a man to complete me and my life. I'm still single and at the age of 60. There is nothing wrong with that. I just haven't found the right man, and I am in no rush.*

5. *Don't try to fix your problems with things of the world like food, money, drugs, or alcohol. Give your problems to God. I'm proud to say I have been drug-free, cigarette-free, alcohol-free for thirty plus years and I'm going strong.*

6. *There is no such thing as a perfect parent. I used to blame myself for not being a better parent, but I have yet to find a perfect one. The only perfect parent is our Father God, and we need to grant ourselves grace.*

7. *I stay on a budget. I found myself in debt from eating out and shopping to feel better. I realized I need to stop spending money to feel good. I only need God to feel good.*

8. *Don't ever sell yourself short. I used to think I had nothing to offer anyone. Now I am blessed with three beautiful grandchildren. It has been my calling to help in raising them, teaching them, and planting seeds of faith in them. I have instilled in my grandson to respect everyone, especially women, and to have pride in all he does. I remind him a hard day's work never hurt anyone. My granddaughters are beautiful inside and out. I love to watch them grow, and I think I am a great teacher.*

9. *Weight loss is a lifestyle change. Focus on being healthy. Focus on different ways to prepare your fruits and vegetables, not the weight you need to lose. That will come and be an ongoing lifestyle change.*

10. *I need to love myself. I learned that I'm important, and I need to take time for myself.*

11. *Keep your eyes on God. Remember no matter how dark things seem, God is bigger and brighter. He can't force us to have a relationship with Him. We must seek Him on our own. Through seeking Him, your life will never be the same.*

12. *Continue Standing Up!! If you fall off the wagon, get up and dust yourself off.*

13. *Pick your friends wisely. I know it's hard to be alone sometimes. There will be a lot of people who will make comments, some good and some not so good. Ignore it and consider the source. It's sad to say, but you will find out who really cares for you. Some people are not going to be happy with your progress of life changes.*

14. *Stay away from food pushers. I had a very dear friend who knew I was not eating certain foods and would always offer them to me.*

15. *This was a big one for me: Don't join a gym if you are not fully dedicated to going every day. I was stuck in an annual $38.00 a month gym membership. I wasted a lot of money. Walking outdoors is free and enjoyable.*

16. *Don't be a food cop. I had to learn that I cannot force my lifestyle on others. I had to learn to relax and enjoy the ride. To enjoy each day and each meal while not criticizing others.*

17. *Celebrate the small things. Everything you achieve, your small goals for weight loss or a goal you set out to accomplish in your journey—treat yourself to something. If you find out that you're a runner or walker and you trained and are ready for that 5k, treat yourself to a pair of good shoes. If you get them on sale, then I would say go for the socks too.*

18. *Give all your problems to God.*

Matthew 6:25-34

25 *Therefore I tell you, don't be anxious for your life: what you will eat, or what you will drink; nor yet for your body, what you will wear. Isn't life more than food, and the body more than clothing?*
26 *See the birds of the sky, that they don't sow, neither do they reap, nor gather into barns. Your heavenly Father feeds them. Aren't you of much more value than them?*
27 *"Which of you, by being anxious, can add one moment literally, cubit to his lifespan?*
28 *Why are you anxious about clothing? Consider the lilies of the field, how they grow. They don't toil, neither do they spin,*
29 *yet I tell you that even Solomon in all his glory was not dressed like one of these.*
30 *But if God, so clothes the grass of the field, which today exists, and tomorrow is thrown into the oven, won't be much more clothe you, you of little faith?*
31 *"Therefore don't be anxious, saying, 'What will we eat?', 'What will we drink?' or, 'With what will we be clothed?'*
32 *For the Gentiles seek after all these things; for your heavenly Father knows that you need all these things.*
33 *But seek first God's Kingdom and his righteousness, and all these things will be given to you as well.*
34 *Therefore don't be anxious for tomorrow, for tomorrow will be anxious for itself. Each day's evil is sufficient.*

ENCOURAGING THE HEALING PROCESS

1. CHURCH: *Living here in Texas, I never had a church to call my own. Until one Sunday we were going to church and my grandchildren were little and said let's go to this church where they had video games. I thought, "Hmm? video games?" My grandson guided us to a church he had previously attended with his father. Their little hands pointed the way. Once we got there, the door greeter opened the entrance and welcomed us in. It was like if God was telling me, "Welcome home, My child". As we walked around and got the kids checked in, my grandson was right, there were video games, but also bible teachings and activities for the kids. My daughter and I got a seat and the service started. So, did the tears all through worship. I felt like the service the pastor gave was just for me. I had found a place where I belonged. When we got back to the car, I asked my daughter if we could come back Wednesday night to the bible study. Now I am*

proud to say it is "My Church." I think whatever religion you are, this is an important part of healing.

2. COMMUNITY: *It was not till after my mother passed away in September of 2005. I found myself with no friends. My mom was my mother and best friend. Besides her and my daughter, I didn't need anyone else. Making friends was a big learning experience. Sometimes you must just put yourself out there to meet people and get out of your comfort zone, which I found I had to do. Through this process, I have made some acquaintances and great long-lasting friendships through my everyday life activities and through my church family. When you love the world, the world will love you back. Building healthy friendships helped me heal.*

3. VOLUNTEERING: *For me, volunteering is a MUST. It was hard at first, but once I got started, it gave me purpose. I think of all the big and small blessings God gives me every day. In return, why can't I give one hour at church service to give back? I have worked 5+ years in the coffee shop at our church. I do various jobs there, from cleaning, stocking, cash register, and sometimes filling in for the manager if she takes a day off. As of now, I just serve coffee and try to keep the line moving; I pass out a lot of hugs. There is no paycheck for this job at the coffee shop, but at the end of the work shift, it feels rewarding. Volunteering can be anything. It doesn't have to be in the church. It could be checking in on*

*an elderly neighbor. Helping a new mom, giving
her an hour or two of free time. Cooking a meal
for a person who cannot drive, is ill, or doesn't
have a family. Volunteering has helped me heal.*

4. KINDNESS: *It may sound simple, but I like to be kind
to people. Kindness is free. Sometimes when I am
out and about in my daily errands. I make it a point
to hold open the door, greet everyone in my path
with a big smile. If I get the prompting from God, I
pass out hugs and handshakes. My thought in this
was sometimes, in that moment, you never know
what the other person is going through. Sometimes
a kind word or gesture will change a person's day.
Being intentionally kind to others helped me heal.*

5. EXERCISING: *When I do something good for
myself, I feel better. I don't like to spend money
or eat out, so I will go for a walk around the
neighborhood. I love to walk and meditate on
God's beautiful sky and nature. I love to answer
my granddaughter questions, as she points
and says, "What that?" I also give myself
exercise credit for cleaning and decluttering.
Exercising and moving around helped me heal.*

6. COUNSELING: *This is a BIG ONE. If possible, I think
everyone, especially myself have or will benefit from
it. I have always been in counseling, and I have
been blessed with some awesome female counselors.
I chose a female counselor because I felt that they
could relate more to my issues I have had. But let's*

face it, we all have some sort of baggage. Whether it is trauma from childhood abuse, dysfunctional family upbringing, drugs, alcohol, or physical abuse from a partner, anyone can benefit from some type counseling. So, for me as a child when my emotional eating started, I just keep pushing down the emotions with food. Counseling helped me deal with my pain and emotions. As I have deepen my relationship with Christ, I seek him first for counseling. I always pray for God to put the right people in my path, and since the death of my mom in 2005, I have seen the same counselor. There is nothing wrong with seeing a counselor, pastor, or psychologist. I see her 3 to 4 times a month. You might think that's a lot and it must cost a lot, here's is my take on that. One hour goes by fast to get everything out that I have on my mind, and to hear her feedback. To be honest, after I'm done crying and using up all her Kleenex, I leave feeling good. I prefer to spend my money on a counselor than shopping or eating out. That is my preference, and my time with her has helped me heal.

7. *SEE YOUR DOCTOR: I see my doctor regularly for a check-up and blood work. For years and years, I never took care of myself. Now, I love myself and feel the need to take care of myself regularly. Also, take care of your mouth. Your mouth is like the house of cards. When one falls, they all fall. God gave us a body to honor. Honoring my body has helped me heal.*

HOW I TACKLED OVEREATING & WEIGHT LOSS

1. *I had to get to the root of why I was overweight. I had to dig deep and be honest with myself.*

2. *I had to stop being a victim.*

3. *I had to learn to love myself.*

4. *I had to understand that changing my body was a lifestyle, not a temporary diet.*

5. *I had to challenge myself and set goals.*

6. *I had to learn to reflect before I ate. I think about why I am eating. "Am I hungry? Am I bored? Am I upset?"*

7. *I had to research and learn. On my journey, I researched non-inflammatory foods, fruits with low sugar impact, and new healthy recipes. I also research teas and vitamins.*

8. *I cleaned out the kitchen. I donated*

processed, canned, and boxed foods.

9. I held myself accountable by attending weekly weigh-ins.

10. I needed an alternative to emotional eating. Journaling was a major key for me. I learned to write down my emotions for the day, or the emotions I was feeling that made me want to stop and buy a donut.

11. I needed to honest. A big thing that moved the scale for me was honesty. You are only lying to yourself and no one else. No cares if you write in your journal, no one cares if you eat three donuts. You must be honest and care about your life and body. The scale will not go down if you are not honest with yourself.

12. Get rid of your big, comfy clothes. They are like security blanks and will enable you to gain weight.

13. I had to remember there is no quick fix to losing weight. I did not become 500 pounds overnight. Therefore, I had to accept it was going to take time to get the weight off. It was not going to happen overnight, and I had to be at peace with my long journey.

14. I had to drink plenty of water. It helps you to lose weight, it's good for your organs, it keeps your joints moving, gives your energy, helps with constipation, makes your skin look good, fights infection, and gets rid of the bad stuff in your body.

15. I cut back on sugar intake and use raw stevia.

Make sure the package says, "no fillers".

16. *I'm not afraid to try new things and go back to old things. Do what works for you and mix it up.*

17. *I only eat fresh or frozen veggies and fruit. I avoid canned because they may have preservatives and excessive salt.*

18. *I now eat breakfast; it's important. I load up my morning with protein, and it keeps me full and satisfied.*

19. *I have a meal plan. Even if it's for a week or a day, a meal plan is important because it keeps me on track. I prep my meals and salads.*

20. *I eat one salad a day. Salads keep me full and I feel fewer cravings.*

21. *Support is important. Join a Facebook group, support group, or find an accountability buddy on the same journey.*

22. *I try to go to bed by 10:00 pm. When my sleeping habits are bad, my eating is bad.*

23. *I organize the refrigerator and pantry at least once a month. I throw out expired food, clean, and organize.*

24. *I use a small plate. This helps me control what was on my plate and not feel deprived.*

25. *I make it a habit of sitting at the table and engage in conversation. Reconnect with family and turn off cell phones and televisions. I think technology distracts you from enjoying your food.*

26. *I add flowers to the dinner table, and avoid paper plates. Glass plates and flowers make my meals feel special. It is a great way to enjoy your food. I am all about embracing my lifestyle and health changes.*

27. *Always be prepared to not want to cook. We are all human. Be prepared at home with a few frozen meals in the freezer. Read the boxes and check the sodium level and ingredients. Try to find something with no preservative. The more natural the better.*

28. *Don't get overwhelmed. Tackle one goal at a time. For example:*
   WEEK 1, Clean out the pantry and donate food.
   WEEK 2, See the doctor.
   WEEK 3, Download a podcast app and research podcast.
   WEEK 4, Find three new recipes.
   Any progress is good.

29. *I had to be realistic. I became an 80-20 club member. It's where 80% of the time you eat healthy food and give yourself grace 20% percent of the time. Allow yourself some space to breathe and eat some fun food with moderation in mind.*

30. *I am a friend to myself. Would you talk negative to a friend or give a friend something unhealthy? No, you would show yourself love and kindness. Always stay positive and true to yourself. Be good to yourself.*

31. *I must keep moving. I learned a Fitbit or step tracker was an important part of my journey. It's a great way to collect data, push yourself to be more active.*

32. *It's ok to reclaim your "why." Maybe when you started your weight loss journey, you did it to get off medication and you achieved that. It's ok to stop and reflect and establish another reason why. I was a size 26-28, and those pants were getting tighter and tighter. I had just left the doctor office for my lab follow-up. I was 275 pounds. I did not want to be 300; I was scared to become 500 pounds, again.*

33. *There is no end to your journey, no crossing the finish line. There are rest stops, but there is nowhere you get off to as a final destination. We need to love the bodies that God has given us because He intended for us to honor and love our bodies. I had to accept honoring my body is an ongoing journey.*

MY DAILY FOOD HACKS THAT MAKE EATING HEALTHY EASIER

Food hacks are little things I do to make eating healthier and easier.

1. *Cut up veggies and fruit ahead of time. For example, I cut different vegetables like onions and peppers. Then, I store them in plastic containers. I use them in my eggs and stir-fry.*

2. *On grocery day, I buy plenty of apples, sugar-free gelatin, and bananas, if I have a sweet tooth those are my go-to snacks.*

3. *I buy a lot of frozen mixed veggies. They are already prepared and ready to cook.*

4. *I like to try new seasoning to put on my veggies. McCormick and Webber have some good seasonings. Make sure you use only a little because of the salt.*

5. *I keep water bottles and apples in my purse to prepare for hunger. One of my main rules is when I leave the house, I must have two apples and two bottles of water in my purse. This keeps me full and helps detour me from stopping at a fast food restaurant.*

6. *I eat a lot of "free" veggies like lettuce and cucumbers. They are low in calories and fill me up.*

7. *I don't buy things I shouldn't eat. For example, I don't buy soda, juices, or chips. My thought on this is if it's in the house, I'm going to be the one to eat it all and if I do want a soda, which is rare. I usually go with a zero calorie or sugar-free soda water. All these years I thought I was hooked on the soda itself. It was actually the carbonation of the drink, so I had no real problem kicking it once I figured that out and switched over to club soda to get rid of the habit.*

8. *I drink a lot of water and green tea. I prefer green, hibiscus, and moringa tea. All three teas are good for your body.*

9. *I am not scared to try new things. I look up recipes and try new spices or brands to mix things up.*

10. *I love raw baby spinach. I add it to everything, including my salads and smoothies.*

11. *It can be difficult to tell what food is good and which is bad. My truth is there is no bad food. It's only when you eat too much of the good food that it becomes bad.*

12. *I love cactus or also known as nopales. I boil them with some salt and a little vinegar to get the goo off of them. Drain them and then sauté them with fresh onion and tomatoes chopped up. Then, I serve them on the side of my meal, warm them up and make a taco out of them, add a cup to my bowl of bean soup, and scramble an egg with extra veggies. Anything you can think of, you can do. They are good cooked or raw, depending on how you like them. And they are good for you.*

13. *Most mornings, I like 2 scrambled egg tacos using corn tortillas. I add onion and spinach, or sweet baby bell peppers and add a tablespoon of jack cheese or feta. This is my fast and easy go-to breakfast.*

14. *Peanut butter on a rice cake. I use one tablespoon is a serving of peanut butter. Sometimes I just want an old-fashioned peanut butter sandwich, checking the serving size and calories and sugar-free jelly. Check the serving size with the diet bread especially if you are using 2 slices of bread.*

15. *I love sweet baby bell peppers cut open in half with plain hummus or any flavored hummus. This is an easy snack to prepare.*

16. *Something new I found at the local corner drug store is a graze box. It contains dried black cherries and almonds raw and 3-4 pieces of dark creamy chocolate. That is my evening treat.*

17. *I love stir-fry. My favorite is Mexican squash, calabaza. I chop that with onion and tomato*

and seasoned lightly with garlic salt.

18. *Another stir fry I make is fresh green beans sautéed with fresh sliced mushrooms and onions. Stir fry can be anything you want it to be. By experimenting, you will figure what different combinations of vegetables you will like.*

19. *An old fashion sandwich. It could be lunch meat or tuna, but you must check the serving size and calories. I use light mayo or yogurt and a diet bread or make it in a lettuce wrap. An old-fashioned grilled cheese, toasted in a pan with zero calorie butter or olive oil spray (light spray) on the outside of bread slice, then a thin slice cut of cheese. With my sandwich, I usually have some carrot sticks. If I'm feeling like living on the edge, I will measure out some chips and count them to serving size.*

20. *I love apples, gala or jazz apples are my favorite. I also like Honeycrisp, but they are huge, I can only eat less than half. The trick to the apple is it will last longer and seem like more to eat if you cut it up rather than trying to eat it whole.*

21. *I love beans and rice. I throw them together in a bowl; it's my comfort food. I measure that out and place in containers to freeze. The serving is ½ cup of beans and 1/3 cup of rice. It might seem like nothing, but it's a lot. And I limit that little meal to just on Tuesdays and Thursdays because too much of a good thing can tip the scale.*

22. *Family and I are fans of an old-fashioned treat,*

sugar-free gelatin and pudding. We are always making it and always have it in stock. My trick to the gelatin is I use it as a treat to myself for an accomplished goal. I purchase special containers and they come with lids and are a half cup serving and that is the allowed serving size. I sometimes add fruit or top with a tablespoon of sugar free dairy whip.

23. *I love to eat Greek yogurt. I found that the small containers with fruit flavor that sell for about a dollar, when on sale in the market. I also found out some are high in sugar. So, as I started to read labels more. I now go for s plain full-fat Greek yogurt and added my own fresh berries. Then one day, I decided I wanted a little more sweetness, and I found a jar of sugar-free jelly in the refrigerator. It has no sugar but also low in calories for 1-2 tablespoons, depending on brand.*

24. *By comparing labels, I found that old-fashioned oatmeal is better for you instead of the quick oats. If you are not a fan of Steel cut oatmeal, you can add berries and fruit to it. My mom used to say it sticks to your ribs. I think what she meant was that it stayed with you and keep you full longer. Try to stay away from the instant pre-packaged oatmeal, especially because it is more processed and may have a lot of extra sugar. You should only choose items with 5 grams of sugar or less is my rule of thumb.*

LITTLE BITS OF HAPPINESS

*O*ne of the biggest mistakes in my life was trying to control my life instead of giving it to God. These are the small things in life that bring happiness, but ultimately only God can complete us and make us happy. I wanted to share them with you.

1. *God and his unconditional love for me makes me happy.*

2. *Going to church with my family makes me happy.*

3. *Volunteering makes me happy.*

4. *Giving and receiving hugs makes me happy.*

5. *My family makes me happy.*

6. *The laughter of my grandchildren, even if they are laughing at me, makes me happy.*

7. *Being able to laugh at myself makes me happy.*

8. *A surprise bag of apples from the grocery store makes me happy.*

9. *A trip to the beach with my family makes me feel close to God while looking out at the water. I have peace in my heart as I watch the grandkids. The beach makes me happy.*

10. *To never stop learning about my journey. Learning about myself makes me happy.*

11. *I love to listen to a good podcast. I have several on my iPhone; from diet to spirituality. Podcasts make me happy.*

12. *My social media communities, groups, and supporting people that have become a part of my journey make me happy.*

13. *Time with my friends over a good cup of coffee makes me happy.*

14. *Taking a walk on a beautiful day with my granddaughter, answering all her "what's that?" questions, makes me happy.*

15. *Finally, you the reader who has taken the time to read this humble story about my humble life makes me happy. This journey has not been an easy one. Yet you have taken an interest to understand my life and what I have gone through. That makes me happy.*

Thank you.

IN CONCLUSION,

*T*hank you for letting me share my story and for being part of my healing process. Before I close, I want to share one last bible scripture I love.

It is Philippians 4:4-7.

4 *Rejoice in the Lord always! Again, I will say, "rejoice!"*
5 *Let your gentleness be known to all men. The Lord is at hand.*
6 *in nothing be anxious, but in everything, by prayer and petition with thanksgiving, let your requests be made known to God.*
7 *And the peace of God, which surpasses all understanding, will guard your hearts and your thoughts in Christ Jesus.*

Book Excerpt From:

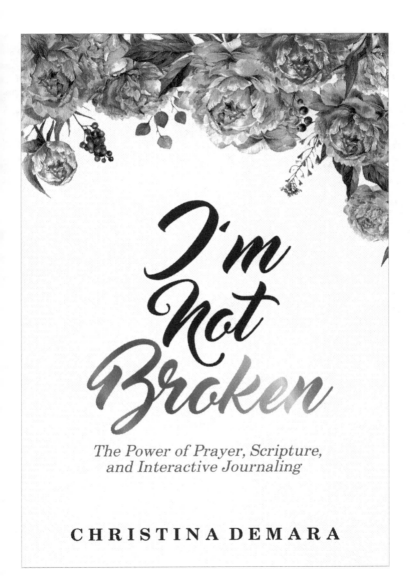

I'm Not Broken

The Power of Prayer, Scripture, and Interactive Journaling

CHRISTINA DEMARA

- 19 -
Heaven

Heaven Defined: The earthly things that bring love and delight.

Let me tell you a story about my grandmother. She was in love with a man named Tom. He was a tall, classy, Caucasian man. They spent time together walking around and talking. But when Tom approached his family about marrying her, he was forbidden. Can you imagine the courage it took for him to ask? I can imagine that deep inside he knew what his family's reaction would be because my grandmother was Hispanic. But, out of love and desperation, he asked for a family blessing. Tom probably had a better chance of getting struck by lightning. My grandmother was devastated. She later married a navy sailor, had four children but suffered at the hand of an alcoholic. There is even a family rumor that when my grandmother went into labor with my mom, she arrived at the hospital with a black eye. I only knew my grandmother at her best. She took care of and prayed for everyone who crossed her path.

She later was diagnosed with Alzheimer's disease. After a long fight, she was hospitalized and was given days to live. She called from the hospital one day, eager and smitten, and asked me to take her to buy a wedding dress. I humored her and went to see her that day after work. She asked me again. Like a little girl, she described her dress and knew the exact place she wanted it from. My mom was visiting my grandmother at the hospital. She just looked at me and gestured to me with her body to go along with it. I replied, "Yes, Grandma, of course, I will take you." She tried to get up, exclaiming that she did not want to be late. She was in a rush all of a sudden. I stopped her before she could get out of her hospital bed. I asked her, "Where do you think you are going?" She said innocently, "I have to get my dress. Tom is coming for me." You see, Tom was her heaven. It was a love that never died. It was a love that she held onto. In my heart, I see her young and beautiful again running away with him in a lace wedding dress. I can see her laughing and smiling. After all the abuse, my grandmother had gone through, she deserved to be happy.

We all have a heaven. Something that brings us peace and keeps us going. For some people dying and going to heaven is a scary thing. There are many people who fear dying for many reasons. Some people fear the unknown, some people fear dying and leaving loved ones behind, and some fear death because they just aren't ready. Although we live here on earth with wars and famine, heaven is all around us. We see it in the sky and the ocean. We see it in the birth of a baby. Heaven is all around us if we choose to see it. It is the same way with the pottery. You can see it as broken, or you can see it as a piece of art.

ABOUT THE AUTHOR

Christina DeMara is passionate about her relationship with God, Jesus, and the Holy Spirit. Christina loves writing books, worship music, learning, leading, teaching, and living life significantly. She is the creative mind behind the coined leadership theory titled Early Life Leadership Infusion. She holds three master's degrees from the University of Texas: one in Special Education, one in Educational Administration and Leadership, and one in Curriculum and Instruction. She later studied business and leadership extensively for six years through Our Lady of the Lake University in San Antonio, Texas. Christina is best known for her creative concepts found in the Early Life Leadership in Children, Early Life Leadership in Girls Workbook, and her Christian books titled Peace Is Mine, The I Am Journal, I'm Not Broken, The Power of Prayer, Scripture, and Interactive Journaling.

Christina DeMara has overcome many obstacles in life through the grace of God and tries every day to motivate others. She enjoys spending time with her family, going to the beach, church, cooking, research, teaching, do-it-yourself projects, and trying new restaurants.

Christina has Facebook groups called:

I Love Reading and Writing
&
I Love Leadership!

You are welcome to join!

LET'S STAY CONNECTED!

ChristinaDeMara@gmail.com
ChristinaDeMara.com
EarlyLifeLeadership.com

Follow Christina!
She would love to hear from you.

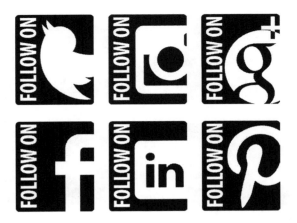

Made in the USA
Columbia, SC
21 January 2025